EXPLORING OUR SOLAR SYSTEM

SPACE PROBES

EXPLORING BEYOND EARTH

DAVID JEFFERIS

Crabtree Publishing Company

www.crabtreebooks.com

W9-BFA-657

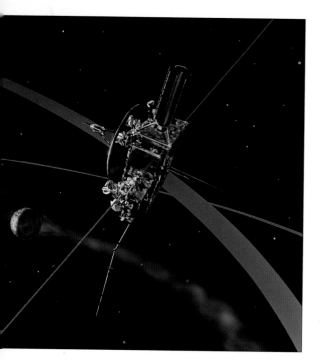

■ ROBOT EXPLORERS

For more than 50 years, space probes have ventured far into the distant parts of the **solar system**. They have revealed the wonders of space, including the hidden secrets of Mercury's craters, the heat-blasted surface of Venus, and the glittering rings of Saturn.

Why should astronomers bother to send space probes at all? There are many scientific reasons, but the real answer is something much deeper. Humans are curious and need to explore new frontiers. Today, robot explorers lead the way!

Crabtree Publishing Company

PMB 16A,
350 Fifth Avenue, Suite 3308
New York, NY 10118

616 Welland Avenue,
St. Catharines, Ontario
L2M 5V6

Published by Crabtree
Publishing Company
© 2009

Written and produced by:
    David Jefferis/Buzz Books
Educational advisor: Julie Stapleton
Science advisor: Mat Irvine FBIS
Editor: Ellen Rodger
Copy editor: Adrianna Morganelli
Proofreader: Crystal Sikkens, Katherine Berti
Project editor: Robert Walker
Prepress technician: Margaret Amy Salter
Production coordinator: Margaret Amy Salter

■ ACKNOWLEDGEMENTS
We wish to thank all those people who have helped to create this publication. Information and images were supplied by:

Agencies and organizations:
    ESA European Space Agency
    JAXA Japan Aerospace Exploration Agency
    JPL Jet Propulsion Laboratory
    NASA National Aeronautics
        and Space Administration
    Toyota Motors

Collections and individuals:
    Alpha Archive
    David A. Hardy
    Mat Irvine
    David Jefferis
    Emily Stapleton-Jefferis

Pioneer 11 flyby art by Andrzej Mirecki, using Celestia software with add-on by Jack Higgins

Library and Archives Canada Cataloguing in Publication
Jefferis, David
        Space probes : exploring beyond earth / David Jefferis.

(Exploring our solar system)
Includes index.
ISBN 978-0-7787-3724-7 (bound).–ISBN 978-0-7787-3741-4 (pbk.)

    1. Space probes–Juvenile literature. I. Title. II. Series: Exploring our solar system (St. Catharines, Ont.)

TL795.3.J43 2008   j629.43'54   C2008-907016-X

Library of Congress Cataloging-in-Publication Data

Jefferis, David.
    Space probes : exploring beyond Earth / David Jefferis.
        p. cm. -- (Exploring our solar system)
    Includes index.
    ISBN 978-0-7787-3741-4 (pbk. : alk. paper) -- ISBN 978-0-7787-3724-7 (reinforced lib. bdg. : alk. paper)
    1. Space probes--Juvenile literature. I. Title. II. Series.

TL795.3.J445 2009
629.43'54--dc22

2008046249

CONTENTS

■WHAT IS A SPACE PROBE?

Space probes are spacecrafts without crews that explore space beyond Earth. They have studied the Moon, major planets, and other space objects.

■ This view of the solar system shows a range of space probes and their targets.
1 SOHO learns about the Sun.
2 MRO orbits around the planet Mars.
3 Voyager 1 flew by Jupiter and Saturn.
4 Voyager 2 also noted Uranus and Neptune.
5 New Horizons is on its way to Pluto.
6 Cassini explores Saturn and its moons.
7 Galileo studied the giant planet Jupiter.
8 Venus Express orbits the hot planet Venus.
9 Messenger is observing Mercury.

■ WHERE DO SPACE PROBES GO?

Space probes have now visited much of the solar system, but there are other places to go besides planets. Jupiter and Saturn each have systems of many moons, which are fascinating subjects to study.

WOW!
An **orbit** is the curving path a smaller space object takes around a bigger one. A space probe can orbit around a space object, as the Moon orbits the Earth.

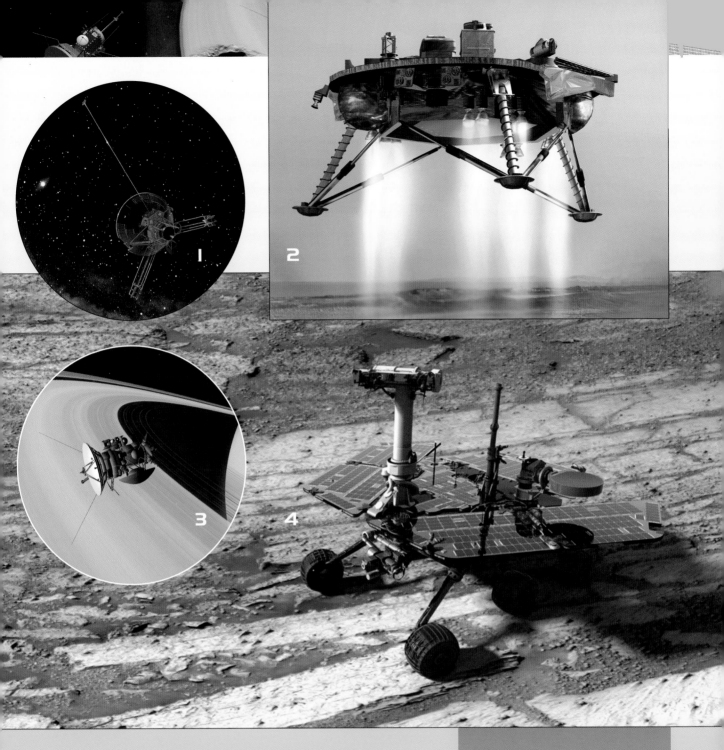

■ ARE THERE DIFFERENT TYPES OF PROBES?

There are several basic kinds. **Flyby** probes go past a space object, studying it briefly as they hurtle onwards. There are two kinds of lander probes: "soft" landers brake to a controlled touchdown using rockets, parachutes, or air bags. An **impactor** lander makes a "hard" landing by crashing straight onto a space object. Orbiter probes circle a planet or other space objects over long periods of time in order to study it in detail. **Rovers** are built to drive around on a planet or moon.

□ Here are examples of four kinds of space probes.
1 Pioneer 10 was a Jupiter flyby probe. It has now moved beyond the planets.
2 Phoenix is a soft lander probe. Its main mission is to find water on Mars.
3 Cassini is a Saturn orbiter.
4 Mars rovers roll along on six metal wheels.

WHEN DID PROBES FIRST GO TO THE MOON?

In 1957, the Space Age began when Russia sent the first spacecraft into orbit around Earth. The next big target was the Moon.

■ The Russian Luna 1 (1) weighed 796 lbs (361 kg). Surveyor 3 (2) was a U.S. lander that helped to prepare the way for crewed Moon flights. The Lunokhods **(3) were very successful Moon rovers.**

WHAT WAS LUNA I?

In 1959, Luna I was the first space probe to fly near the Moon. A launch-rocket error meant that Luna 1 missed the Moon and instead flew past it, about 3,725 miles (5,995 km) away.

WHAT DID ASTRONAUT ALAN BEAN FIND?

He was the **lunar module** pilot of the 1969 Apollo 12 Moon flight (2 above). Bean landed near the Surveyor 3 probe that had touched down almost three years before. The probe checked that the surface was strong enough for humans to land.

WOW!
All the planets except Mercury and Venus have moons, although most are smaller than Earth's single Moon. In all, the solar system has at least 327 moons.

HOW FAR DID THE LUNOKHOD ROVERS GO?

In 1970, two Russian machines, Lunokhod 1 and 2, became the first rovers to study the Moon. Humans had already landed there, but the Lunokhods went on to cover a 30-mile (48-km) area, and take more than 100,000 pictures. Later, more Russian probes were sent to the Moon, and three of these returned to Earth with small soil samples.

□ The Lunar Reconnaissance orbiter (LRO) is a mapping probe. Its mission was to prepare the way for U.S. astronauts to return to the Moon, after 2015. LRO's orbit is a close one, moving just over 30 miles (50 km) above the airless surface.

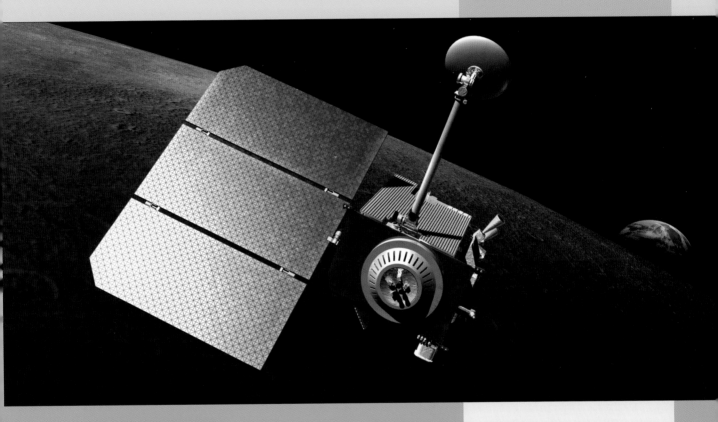

□ Selene was the second Japanese Moon probe. The 6,613-pound (2,999 kg) craft carried 13 instruments, and made movies of its flight using a TV camera.

□ WHAT'S NEXT?

After many years of little interest in Moon exploration, many flights are now planned. The U.S. and Russia are planning new missions. China, Europe, India, and Japan all have space probes going there as well.

■ HOW DO SPACE PROBES STUDY THE SUN?

Probes study the Sun using telescopes, heat sensors, radiation counters, and dozens of other instruments.

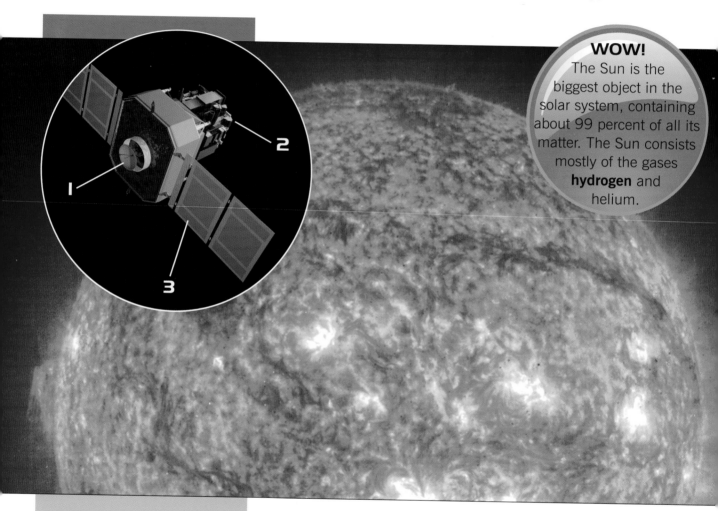

WOW!
The Sun is the biggest object in the solar system, containing about 99 percent of all its matter. The Sun consists mostly of the gases **hydrogen** and helium.

■ SOHO has been in space since 1995, and is still working, despite mechanical problems in 1998. Antennas (1) send information from the onboard instruments (2). Electricity is supplied by solar panel **"wings"** (3).

■ WHAT IS THE SOHO SPACE PROBE?

SOHO stands for SOlar and Heliospheric Observatory. The probe studies the Sun and the **heliosphere**. This is the giant bubble in space filled by the "solar wind"—a stream of invisible particles that pours constantly out of the Sun. SOHO orbits in space 930,000 miles (1.5 million km) from Earth, which gives it a clear view of the Sun.

The Ulysses space probe was built to fly high above and below the Sun. This was to view the Sun's poles, which cannot be seen from Earth. Of course, the Sun's poles are intensely hot—unlike the north and south poles on Earth.

■ WHY DO WE NEED TO STUDY THE SUN?

The Sun is the center of the solar system, and its heat and light allows life on Earth to exist. Studying how the Sun works can help to predict Sun storms and **flares**. Storms and flares can cause electricity black-outs on Earth and can also damage the electronic systems of satellites orbiting Earth.

■ ARE FUTURE SUN PROBES PLANNED?

Yes, the Solar Probe Plus will fly closer to the Sun than any other spacecraft—with a fiery approach of more than four million miles (6.5 million km). Compare this with Earth's distance of about 93 million miles (150 million km)!

■ The Solar Probe Plus will be protected by a nine-foot (2.7-m) heat shield, **to keep it from burning to a crisp.**

■HOW MANY PROBES HAVE BEEN TO MERCURY?

Two space probes have studied Mercury, the planet closest to the Sun. The first was Mariner 10 in 1974–75, followed by the Messenger probe in 2008.

■ WHAT WAS THE MARINER PROBE'S FLIGHT PATH?

Mariner 10 (left) first flew by the planet Venus. It used the **gravity** pull of Venus to bend its course on to Mercury. This "**gravity slingshot**" actually used far less fuel than a direct flight path.

■ **Mercury orbits the Sun at a distance of just 36 million miles (58 million km). This is less than half that of Earth.**

In daytime, Mercury roasts under the Sun's glare. At night, temperatures drop to hundreds of degrees below zero, because the planet has an extremely thin atmosphere, **with no wind to take heat from dayside to nightside.**

■ WAS MARINER'S MISSION A LONG ONE?

After a first flyby in March 1974, Mariner 10 looped past the Sun and returned twice more. During its final flyby in 1975, the probe streaked past, just 203 miles (327 km) above Mercury's surface.

■ WHAT IS MERCURY LIKE ON THE SURFACE?

Mariner 10 took nearly 3,000 pictures of Mercury. The images showed a crater-scarred planet that looks much like the Earth's Moon. In daytime, the airless surface can reach temperatures that are more than double those of the hottest kitchen oven.

WOW!
Mariner 10's gravity slingshot was a space "first." Since then, other probes have used slingshots as a way to gain speed to go to the next target.

Shield protects probe from the Sun's heat

Messenger's mission calls for three flybys, and a year in orbit

Temperatures on Mercury reach up to 800°F (427°C)

WHAT HAS THE MESSENGER PROBE FOUND?

The U.S. Messenger probe was the first mission to Mercury since Mariner 10. The probe sent back its first pictures in 2008. Among the discoveries was a feature named "the spider" (arrowed above). It has a large crater "body," with a network of cracks making the "legs."

BepiColombo is a Mercury probe being developed by teams in Japan and Europe. It will have two orbiters, one close to Mercury, and one flying further out.

HOW DOES A SPACE PROBE FLY TO VENUS?

A mission starts with careful preparation of the probe, followed by attaching it to the launch rocket. After a successful launch, the journey has just begun.

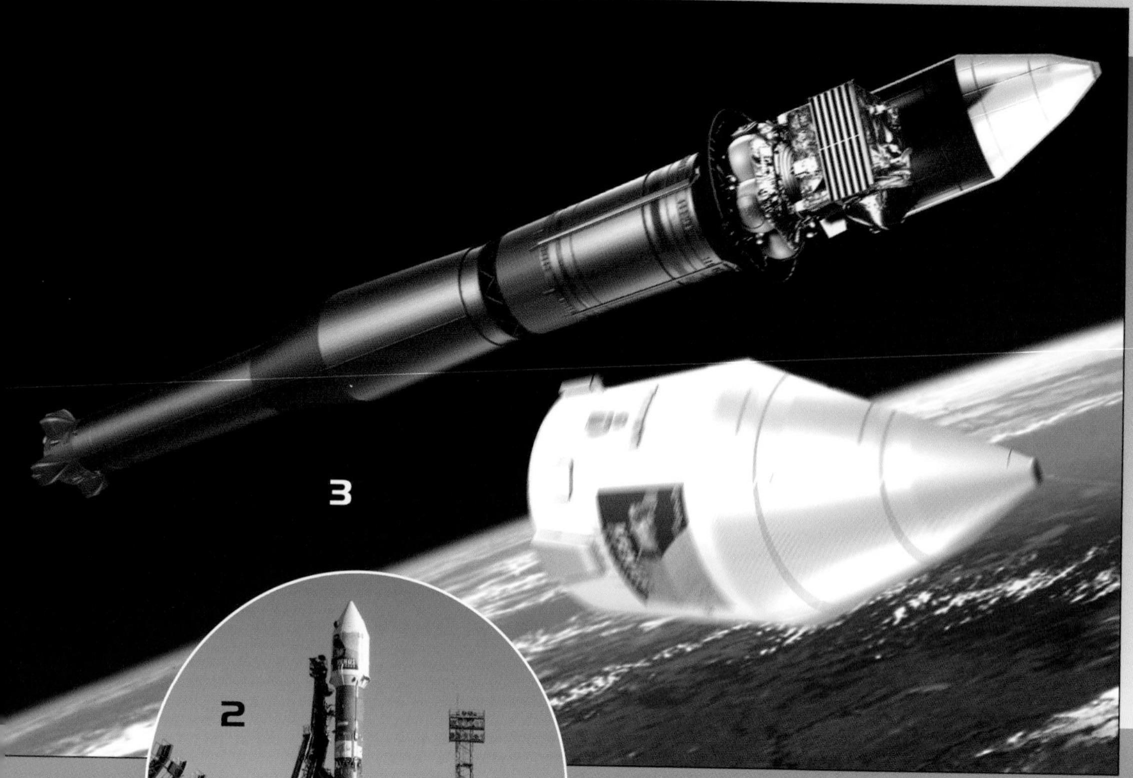

3

2

I

■ A space probe is prepared for flight in a clean room (1). The technician's hair is covered, to avoid any falling into a vital part of the probe. Then the probe is packed carefully aboard the launch rocket (2). High above Earth, the outer casing is ejected (3), ready for the probe to detach.

☐ WHAT IS A CLEAN ROOM?

It is the dust and dirt-free place where a probe is assembled. Space probes are complicated pieces of equipment that have no one to mend them once they leave for another planet. Even a speck of dust in a delicate electronic part can wreck a mission.

☐ HOW MUCH DOES A SPACE PROBE WEIGH?

Weight varies from probe to probe. The one shown here is called Venus Express, and weighs 3,086 pounds (1400 kg). Other space probes have been bigger than this. The Cassini probe, built to survey the planet Saturn, weighed more than 5.9 tons (six tonnes) at launch.

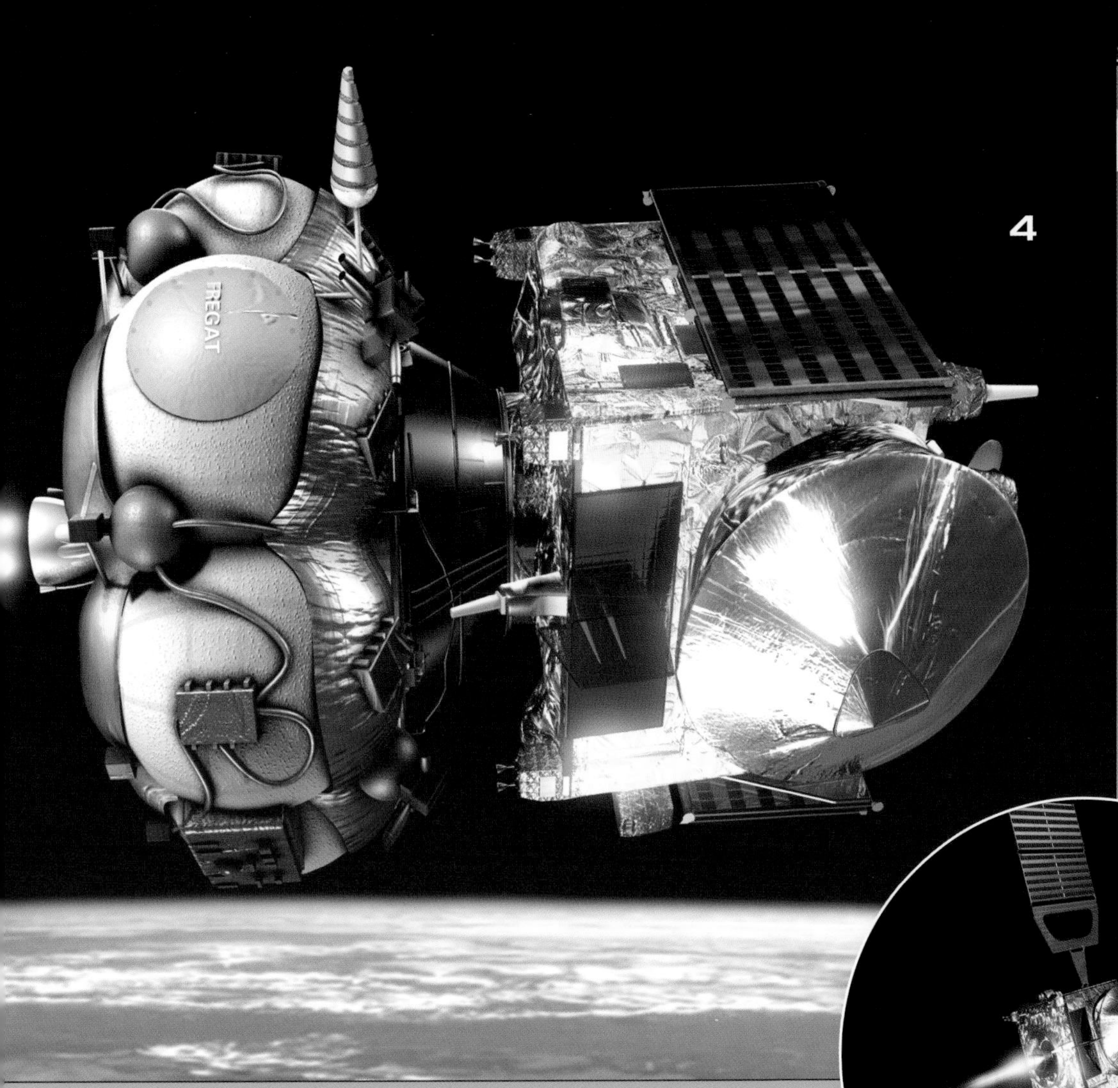

4

■ The thrust for the Earth-to-Venus cruise flight came from the launch rocket's top section, or stage (4). After the cruise, Venus Express went into orbit around Venus (5).

5

6

■ HOW LONG IS A FLIGHT TO VENUS?

Space probes such as Venus Express follow a curving path through space that takes 150 days before going into orbit around the cloudy planet. Venus is the closest planet to Earth, and other journeys take much longer to complete. For example, the New Horizons probe will have been in space nearly 10 years before reaching its flyby target, the cold and distant **dwarf planet** Pluto.

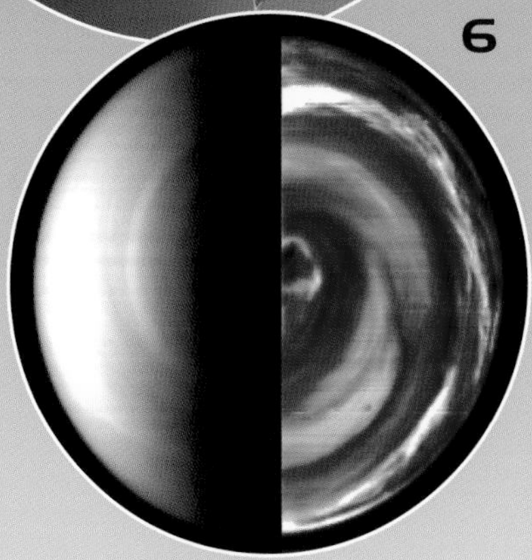

WHAT HAPPENS AT THE DESTINATION?

Venus Express was designed as an orbiter, so the final part of the voyage was to slow down by firing an onboard rocket for 50 minutes. This allowed Venus Express to go safely into orbit around Venus, rather than hurtling past at top speed.

WOW!
The first probe to land on another planet was the Russian Venera 7, in 1970. It crunched down on Venus in 1970, but lasted only 23 minutes in the scorching heat.

■ Instruments on Venus Express study many things, including the hot winds that blow around the planet (6). They are seen here in red, as shown by heat sensors.

WHAT ARE MARS ROVERS?

Rovers are robots that can move around on Mars. They use specially designed wheels that provide a good grip on the dusty surface of the red planet.

■ In 2006, Opportunity halted at the edge of Victoria crater. This crater is millions of years old, and was punched out of the soil when a huge space rock smashed onto the surface.

WHAT ARE THE SPIRIT AND OPPORTUNITY ROVERS?

These are the names of two six-wheel rovers that have explored parts of Mars since 2004. They have drilled for rock samples and have taken thousands of pictures.

WHAT WAS THE FIRST ROVER TO LAND ON MARS?

This was a machine, called Sojourner, that was about the size of a microwave oven. It landed in July 1997, and spent 83 Martian days ("sols") exploring. In fact, Sojourner was not the first robot explorer on Mars. In 1976, two U.S. Viking probes touched down safely, but they had no wheels and stayed where they landed. Their main mission was to test the atmosphere, and dig soil samples to see if there was any life on Mars.

■ Technicians check out the Opportunity rover, before its flight to Mars. The solar panels, which provide electricity, are folded neatly for flight, like flower petals. On Mars, they unfold to form a flat sheet on top of the rover.

■ WHAT HAVE ROVERS FOUND ON THE RED PLANET?

They have spent most of their time studying the rocks, soil, and atmosphere on Mars. Their purpose was to see if Mars has any water. The presence of water means life could have existed there. Scientists believe that the Opportunity rover landed on what had been a coastal area millions of years ago. The landing zone was probably an ancient salt flat on the edge of a shallow sea. The rover's explorations have shown that science fiction martians do not exist.

■ The Mars Surface Laboratory (MSL) is a bigger rover design. Like Spirit and Opportunity, the MSL has cameras mounted on a pole, but uses a power system called an RTG. This is because solar panels are often covered in Mars dust, which reduces the electricity they can generate.

■HOW BIG IS THE MEGAPLANET JUPITER?

Jupiter is far bigger than all the other planets put together. You could fit 1,300 Earths into the same volume as Jupiter and still have room to spare!

■ WHAT WAS THE FIRST JUPITER PROBE?

This was Pioneer 10, which flew past Jupiter in 1973, at a distance of 80,000 miles (130,000 km). It was followed by Pioneer 11 the following year, which went much closer at just 21,000 miles (34,000 km). It then flew on to look at Saturn. Both Pioneers are now far away, drifting toward the outer reaches of the solar system.

■ WHICH WAS THE MOST IMPORTANT PROBE?

This was the Galileo orbiter mission, which arrived in Jupiter's orbit in 1995, after a six-year voyage from Earth. Galileo spent until September 2003 studying Jupiter and its moons. Galileo also carried a smaller probe, which it sent plunging into Jupiter's atmosphere.

■ Here Galileo is being checked out before the flight to Jupiter and its moons.
The cucumber-shaped part sticking up is the main antenna for communicating with scientists on Earth. It was designed to unfold and open out like an umbrella.

A heat shield protected the probe from the fierce heat of entry into Jupiter's atmosphere

■ Galileo released this probe into Jupiter's atmosphere. The 747-lb (339-kg) probe survived for nearly an hour after entry, floating down for 93 miles (150 km), before being crushed by the surrounding gases.

WOW!
The Galileo probe was named after Galileo Galilei, an Italian astronomer. In 1610, he was the first to spot Jupiter's four biggest moons.

Galileo studied the Great Red Spot (1), a huge storm raging in the atmosphere of Jupiter. The antenna for communications with Earth is shown fully open (2). In fact, it stayed slightly closed (3) which meant that some information was lost. Galileo is shown here passing over Jupiter's moon Io, which has many huge volcanoes (4).

■ WHAT HAPPENED TO GALILEO?

Galileo sent back huge amounts of information, including pictures of the **comet** Shoemaker-Levy 9, when it smashed into Jupiter in 1994. In September 2003, Galileo's mission ended when scientists guided it to a fiery end, plunging into Jupiter's atmosphere. This was to avoid the possibility of Galileo ever crashing into any moons, especially Europa. This moon may have a vast water ocean under its icy covering, where scientists think there may be some sort of **alien** life. So they did not want the risk of Earth organisms from Galileo infecting Europa.

■HAS A SPACE PROBE LANDED ON SATURN?

Four space probes have studied Saturn, but none have landed because it has no solid surface. The Huygens probe has landed on Titan, Saturn's moon.

■ **The Pioneer 11 (right) space probe flew past Saturn in 1979. Pictures from Pioneer showed the amazing rings close-up for the first time. The next flybys of Saturn were by two Voyager probes. They flew past in 1980 and 1981.**

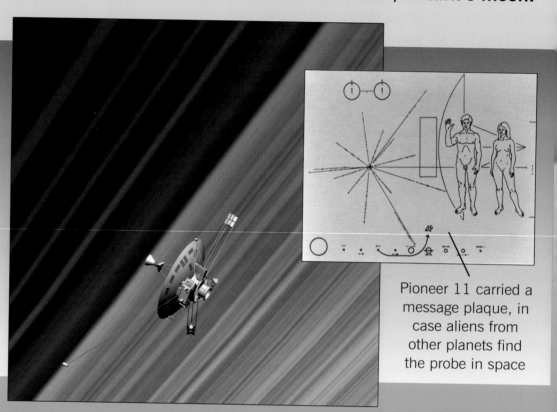

Pioneer 11 carried a message plaque, in case aliens from other planets find the probe in space

■ WHAT DID THE FIRST SPACE PROBE TO SATURN SHOW?

Pioneer 11 led the way to Saturn, which was a largely unknown space zone. Scientists decided to see if the rings were dangerous by aiming Pioneer close to them. Pioneer survived without any damage from ring particles, but nearly hit a previously unknown moon that was only spotted the day before! Pioneer 11 also measured Saturn's **magnetic field**, before heading out into deep space.

WOW!
Titan is the only moon in the solar system to have a thick atmosphere. It is also Saturn's biggest moon, about 50 percent wider than Earth's Moon.

■ WHAT WAS THE CASSINI PROBE'S MISSION?

The Cassini probe was designed to do a number of things—orbit around Saturn, fly by moons, and launch a lander at the big moon Titan.

WHEN DID EUROPE'S HUYGENS PROBE LAND ON TITAN?

The Huygens lander was launched from Cassini, and parachuted safely to the chilly surface of Titan in January 2005. It sent back pictures of a crunchy surface made of pebbles and ice grains, under a smoggy orange sky.

■ Cassini carried the Huygens probe inside a protective "aeroshell" (arrowed). Titan is covered by thick clouds, so no one knew where Huygens would land (top). It was built to survive coming down on flat ground, in mountains, or even floating on the super-chilly surface of a liquid methane ocean. Huygens also had a microphone, which recorded the sounds of Titan's gusty winds.

IS HUYGENS STILL SENDING ANY INFORMATION?

No, the probe had power for only about 90 minutes. Cassini is still studying Saturn and its 60-plus moons, and should do so for many years yet.

■HOW FAR HAVE THE VOYAGER PROBES GONE?

The two Voyager space probes have studied four planets: Jupiter, Saturn, Uranus, and Neptune. Now they are exploring beyond the solar system.

■ WHEN WERE THE VOYAGERS LAUNCHED?

The two identical U.S. probes were fired into space in 1977. There were two launches, 21 days apart. Voyager 1 flew past Jupiter and Saturn. Voyager 2 also visited Uranus and Neptune, in a grand tour of all four outer planets.

■ Each 1,700 lb (772 kg) Voyager was carried into space by a huge Titan 3E Centaur rocket. The Voyagers were equipped for their missions with a mass of instruments that included cameras, radiation counters, and magnetism detectors.

■ WHAT DID THE PROBES DISCOVER?

Among many Voyager findings were new moons, and a close look at Saturn's outer "F" ring. This consists of a ring of small ice particles, with a second, knotted ring spiralling around it!

WOW!
Two Pioneers and two Voyagers are past the planets, and heading to the stars. Pioneer 10 may pass by the giant star Aldebaran, but not for another two million years!

WHAT OTHER FINDINGS DID THE VOYAGER PROBES MAKE?

The big discoveries after the Jupiter and Saturn flybys were Voyager 2's close looks at Uranus and Neptune. Until this mission, astronomers on Earth could only see fuzzy telescope images of the planets.

■ Information about Voyager's various target planets, including Neptune (above) were beamed through the main dish antenna (1). TV cameras and other instruments are carried on a moveable platform (2). Electricity to run the spacecraft comes from an RTG system (3). Magnetometers **are carried on a long metal arm (4). These instruments measure the magnetism in space around the probe.**

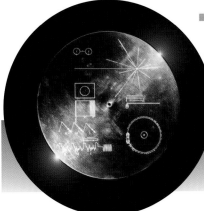

WHERE ARE THE VOYAGERS NOW?

Both probes are moving away from the solar system, and are now studying the heliosphere's outer regions. There should be enough power for their instruments until the year 2025.

■ Like the Pioneer probes, the Voyagers carry a message to possible aliens who may be "out there." As well as pictures, there is also a "Sounds of Earth" audio disk aboard.

■ WHAT LIES BEYOND PLUTO?

The New Horizons probe is heading towards the dwarf planet, Pluto. After this, the next target will be a chilly space zone called the Kuiper Belt.

■ Here the foil-wrapped New Horizons probe is being readied for flight. It left the Earth on January 19, 2006.

■ WHY IS NEW HORIZONS WRAPPED IN FOIL?

Most space probes are covered with layers of thin plastic foil, coated with aluminum or gold. For New Horizons, the foil is a blanket that helps to keep the instruments warm in the intensely cold, outer solar system. Space probes that go nearer the Sun—to Venus or Mercury, for example—need foil for the opposite reason. Foil helps keep instruments cool, by reflecting some of the Sun's heat away from the spacecraft.

WOW!
The speed of light is 186,000 miles per second (300,000 km/sec). Even at this speed, signals from the Pluto zone take four hours 25 minutes to reach Earth.

■ WHEN WILL NEW HORIZONS REACH PLUTO?

As planned, New Horizons will hurtle past Pluto in July 2015. Instruments on the probe should be able to study Pluto and its three moons, Charon, Hydra, and Nix.

Main antenna

RTG power
system

New Horizons has
16 **thrusters** that
allow it to adjust its
course and angle

■ **The
Pluto flyby
will take less
than a day. If all
goes well, New
Horizons will pass within
6,200 miles (10,000 km) of Pluto.**

■ WHAT IS IN THE KUIPER BELT?

The Kuiper Belt is a thinly scattered disk,
far outside the orbits of the planets. It is
thought to contain millions of Kuiper Belt
Objects (KBOs). These are chunks of rock
and ice, ranging in size from boulders
a few feet across, to giants as big as a
small planet. If there are KBOs near New
Horizons, it could be steered toward them.

■ **From the
Kuiper Belt, the
Sun will appear
as little more
than a very
bright star,
giving off little
or no heat.**

■ WHERE ELSE CAN SPACE PROBES EXPLORE?

Humans have already probed much of the solar system. Scientists are still eager to find out more about comets and asteroids.

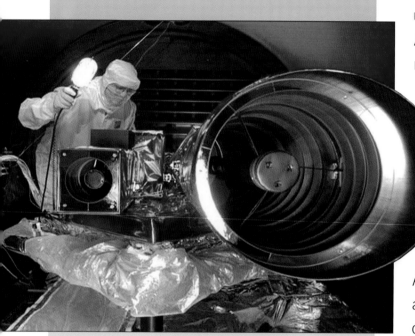

■ In 2005, the Deep Impact probe launched a small impactor probe toward the comet 9P/Tempel. When the impactor hit the comet, the explosion was recorded by Deep Impact's cameras (above).

Main probe

Impactor

Comet

■ WHAT ARE ASTEROIDS?

Asteroids are space rocks, often called minor planets or planetoids. They are thought to be "cosmic rubble," left over after the planets were formed, 4.6 billion years ago. There are thought to be at least 750,000 asteroids. Most orbit the Sun in a belt between Mars and Jupiter.

■ WHAT ARE COMETS MADE OF?

A comet is a loose mixture of ice, dust, and rocks. If a comet drifts near the Sun, the heat may be enough to boil off some of these ices. Then a gas tail streams away, glowing with reflected sunlight.

WOW!
Like Pluto, Ceres is a dwarf planet. It is the biggest object in the Asteroid Belt, about 303 miles (488 km) across. It may have a layer of water under the surface.

■ WHY VISIT THESE SPACE OBJECTS?

Earth's surface is being changed constantly by wind, weather, and other forces, but many asteroids and comets have stayed almost the same for billions of years. Because of this, they are an important key to understanding the early history of the solar system.

As planned, the Rosetta space probe will orbit around its target comet (left). This will allow Rosetta to study the comet's surface.

A small lander (above) should make a gentle touchdown, and using a digging tool, find out what the surface is made of.

WHAT MISSIONS ARE BEING PLANNED?

Several asteroid and comet missions are now in space. The Rosetta probe has already flown by an asteroid, and will send a lander to the comet 67P/Churyumov-Gerasimenko in 2014. The Dawn space probe is on its way to visit the two biggest members of the asteroid belt. The first target is asteroid Vesta, followed by the dwarf planet Ceres.

Dawn will be the first space probe to orbit one space object—Vesta. It will then use its own power to go on to another one—Ceres. To do this, it has an ion drive, a type of motor that runs on electricity from the solar panels.

■ WHERE CAN I LOOK AT SPACE PROBES?

Looking at space probes is not quite as easy as backyard astronomy. For most of us, it means a trip to a museum or a space center.

■ WHAT SHOULD I LOOK FOR IN A MUSEUM?

Many museums have a space gallery, which is the right place to start. If there is a "history of space" section, then the story of space probes should be a big feature. The actual probes are in space or on other planets, so the museum might display life-sized models, or sometimes engineering test rigs.

■ WHAT IS A TEST RIG?

This is a replica probe, built to test how the probe works before it leaves on its mission. The test rig may check that an antenna folds out correctly, or if a digging tool works. Some rigs are placed in test chambers that simulate the extreme conditions of space. This is to make sure the actual probe will work for years to come.

■ This is a life-sized replica of the Giotto space probe, which was aimed by the European Space Agency (ESA) toward Halley's comet in 1986.

The probe successfully flew right through the comet's long, shining tail.

The Giotto probe weighed 1,285 lb (583 kg) at its launch

Solar panels around body of probe

plasma sensing instrument, th
Investigation (PEPSSI), will se
atmosphere and subsequently
solar wind.

...nts, all weighin

■ This is a scaled down (1/25) paper model of the New Horizons space probe. You can make it by downloading the plans and instructions from the Internet. The plans are in color, so all you need to do is cut out the parts and stick them together. The result should be a neat little model like this (right).

Remember that your model is 25 times smaller than the real thing. The probe on its way to Pluto has an antenna nearly seven ft (2.1 m) across! The Internet address for this model is shown on page 31.

■ WHERE DO MUSEUMS GET THEIR SPACE PROBE EXHIBITS?

Many companies in the space industry want to pass on their enthusiasm for what they do and show people their products. Items like this are often supplied free, so people can get an idea of what happens behind the scenes.

■ CAN I MAKE A MODEL SPACE PROBE?

Modelmaking is a great way to dig deeper into this subject, and you can get construction kits of various space subjects. Mat Irvine, who is a science advisor for this book, has written several books on the subject. Look up Mat's name in an Internet bookstore to see what he has written. The cut-out space probe shown above makes a good project. It will look even better than the picture if you make a display for it, with a background of stars, space, and planets.

■ This complex-looking spacecraft is a Russian Venera probe, one of several that went to Venus in the 1970s. It can be seen in the Udvar-Hazy Center, Virginia.

■ FACTS AND FIGURES

■ WHAT WAS THE FIRST SUN SAMPLING PROBE?

This was a space probe called Genesis (right), which was also the first to bring back a sample of anything from beyond the Moon. After a three-year mission in 2004, Genesis crash-landed in the U.S. It brought back tiny samples of the solar wind, which helped scientists understand how the Sun works.

Magnetometer

Jupiter picture taken by the Cassini space probe, while on its journey to Saturn

Each solar panel "wing" is 29.5 ft (9 m) long

Body of Juno spacecraft contains the science equipment

■ WHY IS JUNO THE FIRST JUPITER PROBE TO USE SOLAR CELLS?

Not surprisingly, the strength of sunlight decreases with distance from the Sun. For space probes that go beyond Mars, an RTG power supply is necessary, as it uses heat from plutonium fuel, rather than energy from the Sun.

Solar panels have improved and it is now possible to use them for missions to Jupiter. Even so, Juno's solar panels need to be very big in order to collect enough sunlight.

Main antenna for communications with Earth

Much like a toy gyroscope, Juno spins two to three times a minute for stability in space.

Juno is a very large space probe. This vehicle is shown to the same scale

■ Juno is unusual for its three-solar panel layout. Otherwise it is very similar to most probes. A big dish-shaped antenna is used for radio links with Earth, and is mounted on a body or "bus" that contains small steering thrusters and science instruments.

WHAT WERE THE FIRST SPACE PROBES TO THE PLANETS?

The 1960s were years of much competition between the U.S. and Russia—the world's great space superpowers. Both countries sent missions to Venus and Mars.

Since then, the U.S. has sent space probes to all the major planets. The dwarf planet Pluto is next on the list.

Year	Space probe	Mission	Planet
1962	Mariner 2	Flyby	Venus
1964	Mariner 4	Flyby	Mars
1973	Pioneer 10	Flyby	Jupiter
1974	Mariner 10	Flyby	Mercury
1979	Pioneer 11	Flyby	Saturn
1986	Voyager 2	Flyby	Uranus
1989	Voyager 2	Flyby	Neptune

WHAT IS THE BIGGEST SPACE PROBE ON MARS?

This is the Phoenix lander that touched down in the north polar region of Mars in 2008. With its solar panels unfolded, Phoenix measures 18 ft (5.5 m) across. The science deck in the middle contains the instruments and a digger arm, to take samples of the soil.

WHICH SPACE PROBE HAS GONE FURTHEST FROM EARTH?

Pioneer 10 and 11, and Voyager 1 and 2, are all drifting through space, far beyond the planets. The furthest of the four is Voyager 1, which by 2008, was nearly 104 times further from the Sun than the Earth, or a distance of 9.7 billion miles (15.6 billion km).

GLOSSARY

Here are explanations for many of the terms used in this book.

The first rover probe on Mars was called Sojourner. The rover measured 25 inches (65 cm) in length.

Aeroshell A shell-like structure used to carry and protect a lander.

Alien A word that describes any life from other planets or space areas.

Antenna Any electronic aerial that enables a probe to communicate using radio or TV signals.

Asteroid One of thousands of space rocks that orbit mostly between Mars and Jupiter.

Atmosphere The various gases that surround planets and a few moons.

Clean room An area free of all dirt and dust, where the final assembly of a space probe takes place.

Comet A "dirty snowball" in space, made of ice, dust, and rocks.

Dwarf planet Round space objects, such as Pluto and Ceres, that are smaller than a major planet.

Flare A violent explosion on the Sun.

The outer regions of the heliosphere (arrowed) are being explored by the Voyager space probes.

Flyby A space mission in which a probe goes past a planet rather than landing on it or going into orbit.

Gravity The force of attraction between all objects. Big objects. have a stronger gravitational pull

Gravity slingshot A flight path in which a probe passes a planet closely, on its way to another. The planet's gravity speeds the probe up, giving it a speed boost.

Heat shield A heatproof structure, designed to protect a spacecraft.

Heliosphere The huge bubble in space, filled by particles blown from the Sun, called the "solar wind."

Hydrogen The most common substance in the universe, followed by helium. These two gases make up more than 98 percent of the Sun.

Impactor A space probe designed to crash into a moon or planet.

Kuiper Belt Space zone beyond the planets, in which millions of space objects orbit the Sun.

Lunar Module Two-man spacecraft used for the Apollo Moon landings.

Lunokhod A Russian rover. The name means "Moonwalker."

Magnetic field Area affected by a planet's magnetism.

Part of the Sun to the same scale as the planets

1 2 3 4   5   6   7   8

Magnetometer Instrument that measures the amount of magnetism in surrounding space.

Methane On Earth, a flammable natural gas. Saturn's moon Titan is so cold that methane exists there only as an extremely chilly liquid.

Moon A natural satellite of a planet or dwarf planet. The Moon is Earth's natural satellite. A probe that orbits a planet or other space object is an artificial satellite.

Orbit, orbiter Curving path of one space object around a bigger one.

Radiation The whole range of wave energy in nature, including radio waves, heat waves (infrared), x-rays, and visible light.

Rover Probe that moves around on the surface of a planet or moon.

RTG A power system that supplies electricity, using heat rather than solar power. RTG is short for "radioisotope thermoelectric generator."

Solar panel A flat panel made with silicon. This is a material that changes the energy in sunlight to electricity.

Solar system The name for the Sun, the eight major planets, several dwarf planets, thousands of asteroids, millions of comets, and countless other space objects that circle it.

Thruster A small gas jet on a space probe. Several are used, so that a spacecraft's angle in space can be adjusted accurately.

■ GOING FURTHER

Using the Internet is a great way to expand your knowledge of space probes and other spacecraft.

Your first visit should be to the site of the U.S. space agency, NASA. Its site shows almost everything to do with space, from the history of spaceflight to the universe in general.

There are also websites that give detailed space information. Try these sites to start with:

www.nasa.gov — A huge space site.
www.space.com — Space news site.
lasp.colorado.edu/~hoxie — Site to download the New Horizons model.

■INDEX

Printed in the U.S.A.—C